MY LIFE IN 2055

MY HOUSE IN 2055

CARRIE LEWIS AND CHRISTOS SKALTSAS

Lerner Publications ◆ Minneapolis

Copyright © 2021 by Lerner Publishing Group

All rights reserved. International copyright secured. No part of this book may be reproduced, stored in a retrieval system, or transmitted in any form or by any means—electronic, mechanical, photocopying, recording, or otherwise—without the prior written permission of Lerner Publishing Group, Inc., except for the inclusion of brief quotations in an acknowledged review.

Lerner Publications Company
An imprint of Lerner Publishing Group, Inc.
241 First Avenue North
Minneapolis, MN 55401 USA

For reading levels and more information, look up this title at www.lernerbooks.com.

Main body text set in Mikado a Light
Typeface provided by HVD Fonts

Library of Congress Cataloging-in-Publication Data

Names: Lewis, Carrie (Children's author), author. | Skaltsas, Christos, illustrator.
Title: My house in 2055 / Carrie Lewis ; illustrated by Christos Skaltsas.
Description: Minneapolis : Lerner Publications, [2021] | Series: My life in 2055 | Summary: "What might we see in the house of the future? New materials outside, such as bamboo concrete and green roofs, create pleasant, sustainable dwellings, while robots clean and cook the perfect meal for each resident"— Provided by publisher.
Identifiers: LCCN 2020023905 (print) | LCCN 2020023906 (ebook) | ISBN 9781728416298 (library binding) | ISBN 9781728423548 (paperback) | ISBN 9781728418537 (ebook)
Subjects: LCSH: Ecological houses—Juvenile literature. | Sustainable living—Juvenile literature.
Classification: LCC TH4860 .L488 2021 (print) | LCC TH4860 (ebook) | DDC 643/.10286—dc23

LC record available at https://lccn.loc.gov/2020023905
LC ebook record available at https://lccn.loc.gov/2020023906

Manufactured in the United States of America
1 - 48861 - 49196 - 7/23/2020

TABLE OF CONTENTS

REAL OR IMAGINARY? 4
WELCOME TO MY HOME! 5
OUR HOUSES ARE FLEXIBLE AND SUSTAINABLE! 6
YOU DON'T HAVE TO FLICK A SWITCH 12
WE COOK AND CLEAN DIFFERENTLY, AND WITH
SPECIAL HELPERS! 16
WE ARE EFFICIENT WITH WATER AND ENERGY! 20
WE USE HEAT FROM THE CENTER OF THE EARTH! ... 24
WE GROW OUR OWN FOOD 26
WE LIVE TOGETHER AND SHARE 28

Glossary	30
Learn More	31
Index	32

REAL OR IMAGINARY?

In this book, we're taking a look at the future of houses.

People are always coming up with ideas to make their homes better to live in. Some ideas don't take off—but some change our lives forever.

Homes of the future may look like the ones in this book—but then again, they might not!

While you are reading, pause and think about what you've read. What would your home of the future be like?

WELCOME TO MY HOME!

On the outside, it probably looks like any other house.

It doesn't have anything like a landing pad for spaceships, or a time portal where the door should be. Those things are just in movies.

However, there are some differences in 2055.

This house has grass on the roof. The grass works as insulation and means that butterflies and insects have more places to live.

Also, the garden is full of vegetables and wildflowers. That's because in 2055 we like to grow things ourselves.

LET'S FIND OUT SOME MORE ABOUT HOUSES IN 2055.

OUR HOUSES ARE FLEXIBLE AND SUSTAINABLE!

This house is made from bamboo concrete.

Bamboo is the long, stiff grass that pandas eat. It has very strong fibers. When mixed with resin, it makes a strong material that's great for building.

Bamboo absorbs carbon dioxide in the air, so growing bamboo in farms helps the climate. Don't worry though—when it gets made into concrete, there is still plenty for the pandas because it grows really fast!

In 2055 there are other ways to build new houses. Some houses are built from sandstone using 3D printers.

3D printing is also a quick way to build houses in an emergency. When there's a flood, houses can be printed so that there is shelter for any people who have lost their homes.

Ever wanted to live in a toadstool like a fairy or a gnome?

Some houses in 2055 are built using a substance called mycelium. Mycelium comes from mushrooms! When it is grown in large quantities and made into bricks, it is stronger than concrete.

You don't have to go high-tech to build your home. Some new houses are made with straw bales piled on top of one another and then plastered over. This keeps a house very warm, and you can gather the building materials from anywhere.

A new generation of amazing man-made materials like graphene are also being used for buildings. Graphene is a supermaterial. It's superthin and superstrong, plus it is a superconductor!

In 2055, many houses and apartments are small. This is because a lot of families are just two or three people. Quite a lot of people live by themselves.

Our houses are flexible. We can change things on the inside. Walls can slide backward and forward so that rooms can change size. We can split one big bedroom into two small bedrooms by sliding a wall along on rollers. We could have one big open space or a separate kitchen.

We can change the colors too. Patterned rollers on the walls mean that no one has to paint and decorate. We don't have drapes because the windows tint when it gets dark outside.

11

YOU DON'T HAVE TO FLICK A SWITCH

In 2055, we don't have many outlets, because charging is wireless. Most electronics charge with Wi-Fi from pads that are hidden in the walls.

If you leave your phone on the arm of the sofa near a charger, it will recharge itself just like magic!

A home computer runs most of the gadgets in the house. The computer makes things much more convenient.

Motion sensors respond to the infrared energy given off by our bodies to turn lights on and off. These sensors make our energy use much more efficient because we can't leave the lights on by accident.

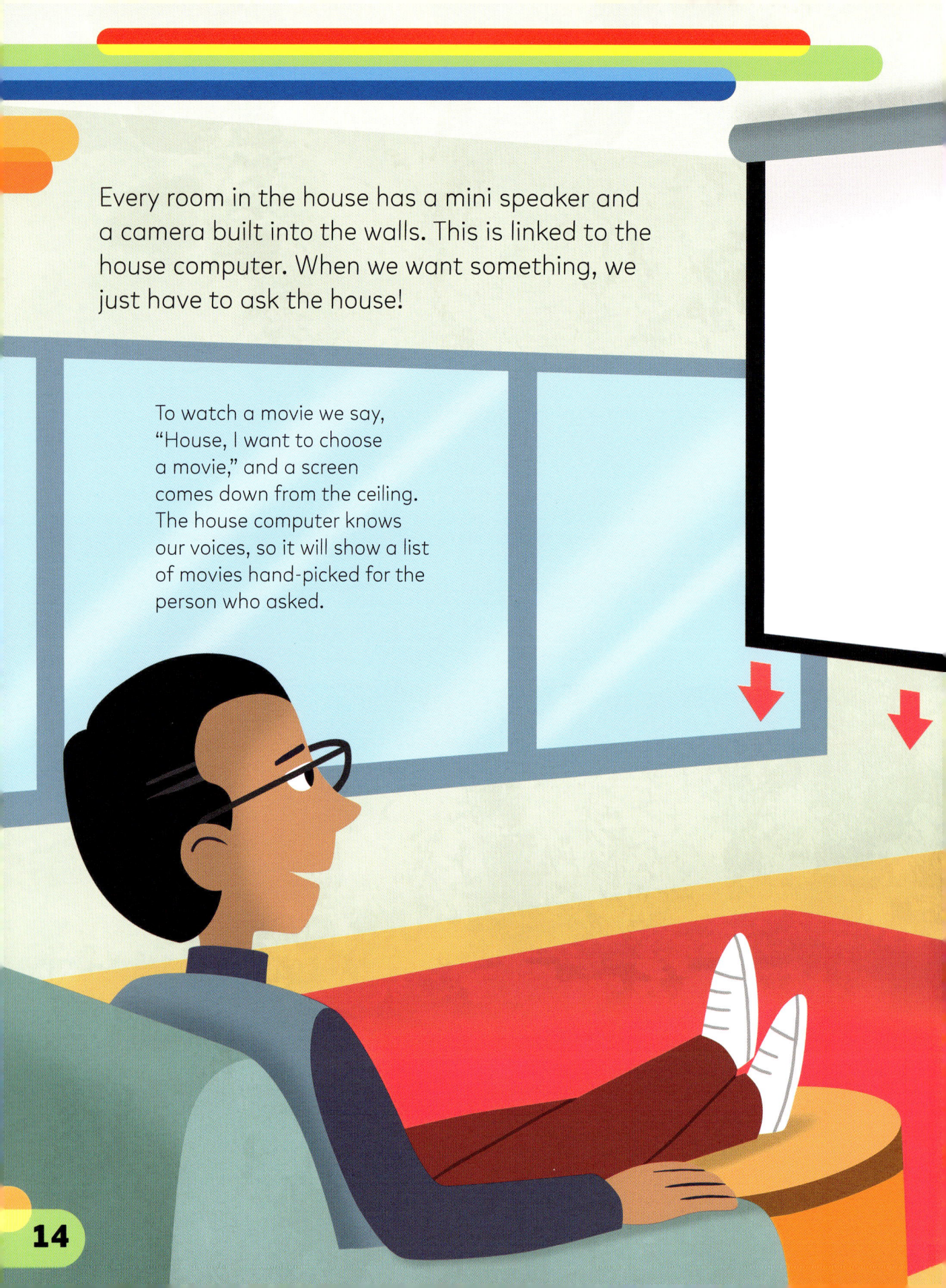

Every room in the house has a mini speaker and a camera built into the walls. This is linked to the house computer. When we want something, we just have to ask the house!

To watch a movie we say, "House, I want to choose a movie," and a screen comes down from the ceiling. The house computer knows our voices, so it will show a list of movies hand-picked for the person who asked.

The house can also see us. When we arrive on the doorstep, we don't need a key to get in. A retina scanner scans our eye with a low-energy infrared beam.

If the house doesn't recognize the person on the doorstep, it rings the doorbell.

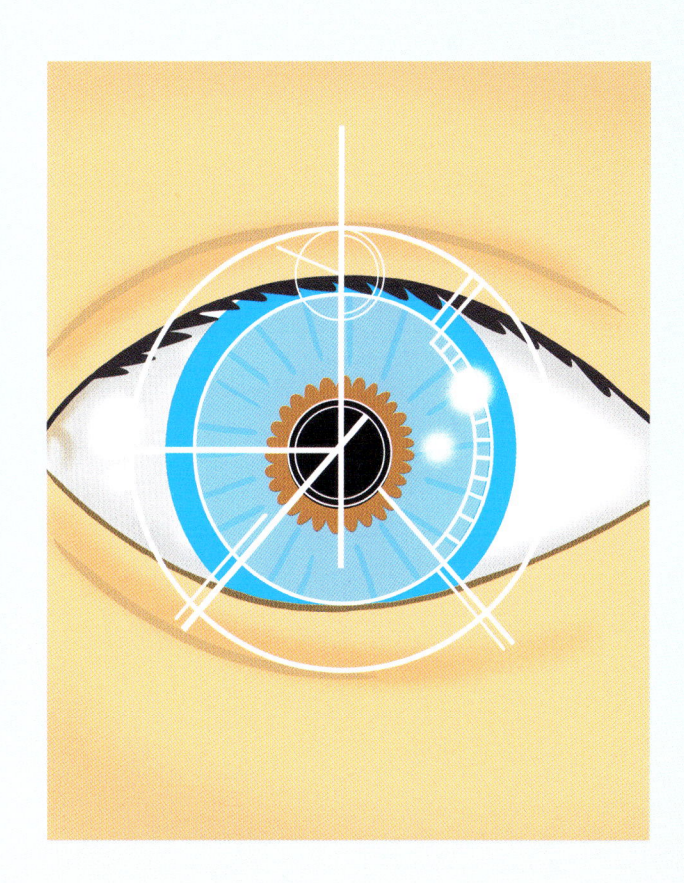

WE COOK AND CLEAN DIFFERENTLY, AND WITH SPECIAL HELPERS!

In 2055, our kitchens have stoves, but these are divided into little pods so that each person can have their own meal, even if they need to be cooked at different temperatures.

We know that different people need different food to be healthy. One person might need a lot of protein, and someone else might need a lot of fiber. By having flexible kitchens that can cook more than one meal at a time, everyone gets what they need.

In 2055, a food mixer can move and talk!

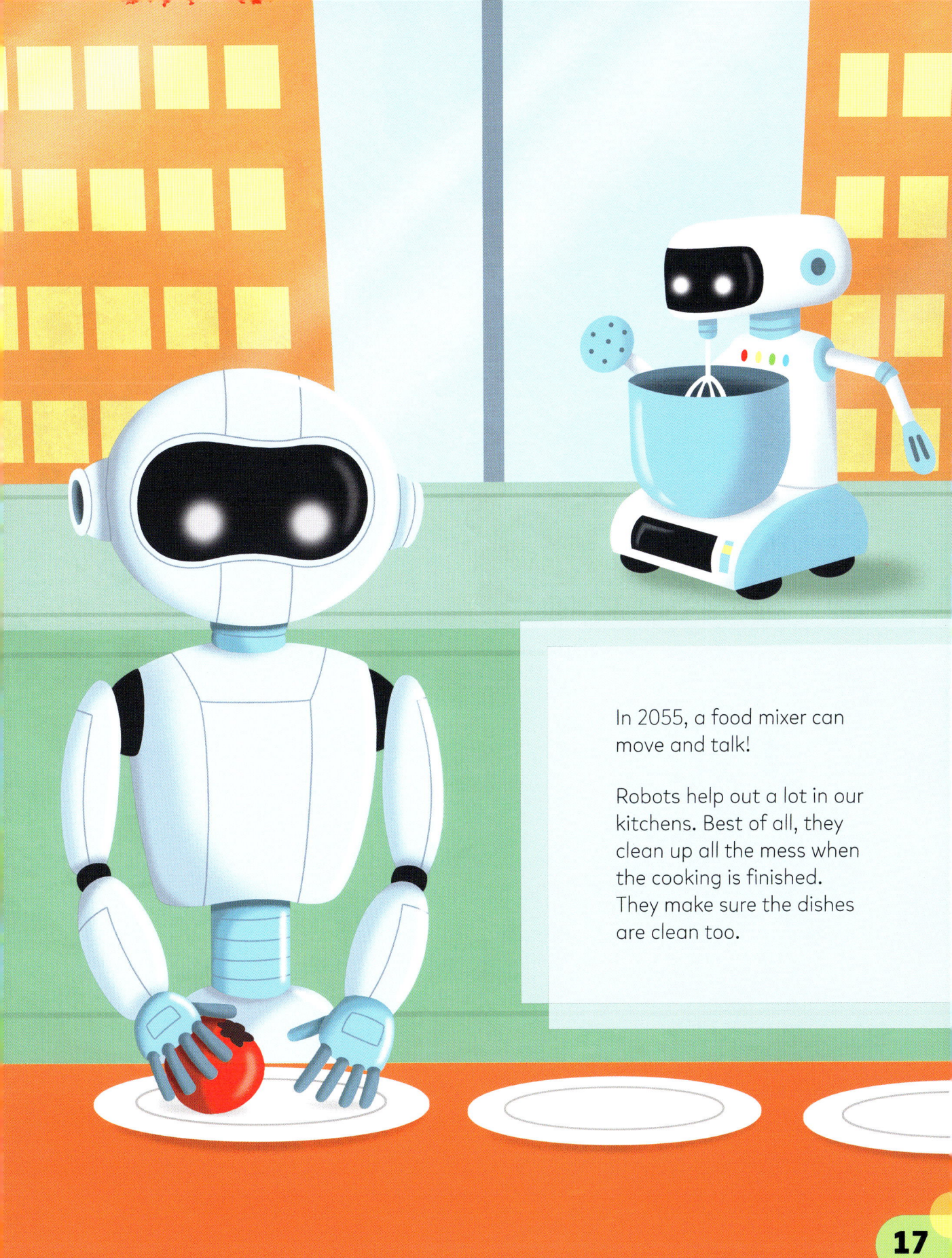

Robots help out a lot in our kitchens. Best of all, they clean up all the mess when the cooking is finished. They make sure the dishes are clean too.

Everyone is busy these days. We like to spend our free time relaxing—not cleaning.

When there is housework to do, the robots do it for us. We have one robot that can dust, polish, and clean the kitchen and bathroom. It has tracks on the bottom like a tractor and it can go up and down the stairs.

A vacuuming robot lives in the closet. When it vacuums, all the dirt goes straight down a chute that's built into the wall.

Robots are helpful for elderly people. They can help with the housework, but they can also make sure that someone has taken their medicine. A robot can be a companion who can call for help if an older person has an accident.

WE ARE EFFICIENT WITH WATER AND ENERGY!

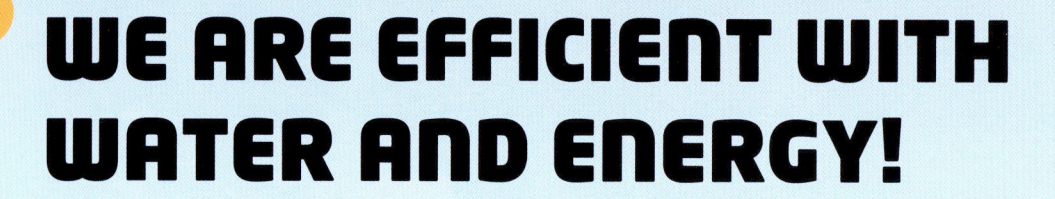

We have a big water tank in the yard. This is for collecting rainwater. The rainwater is used around the house and garden.

We use it to flush the toilet and to wash our hands. We also use it to water the plants in the garden when the weather is dry.

We try not to use too much water because in some places there isn't enough clean water to go around. Because of this, houses are designed to be water-efficient. The faucets turn off automatically when we stop using them. We also try to wash our clothes with as little water as possible, making sure that the washing machine is always full before we turn it on.

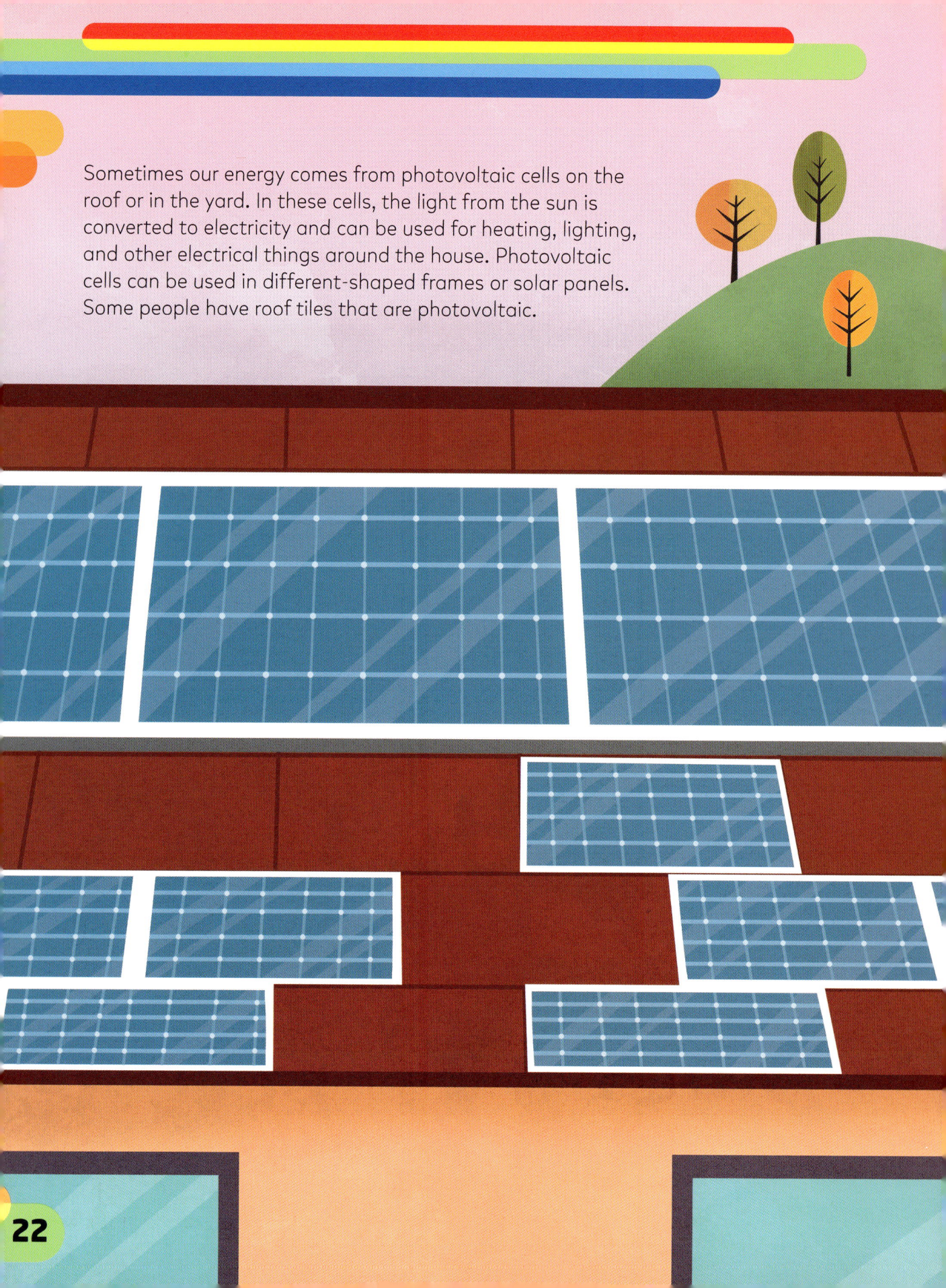

Sometimes our energy comes from photovoltaic cells on the roof or in the yard. In these cells, the light from the sun is converted to electricity and can be used for heating, lighting, and other electrical things around the house. Photovoltaic cells can be used in different-shaped frames or solar panels. Some people have roof tiles that are photovoltaic.

Some homes produce energy from wind. The wind passes through a turbine with a windmill at the top, and this energy is converted to electricity.

When energy has been produced using light or wind, it can be stored for later use or shared among other people.

23

WE USE HEAT FROM THE CENTER OF THE EARTH!

Some people use geothermal heating around the house. Geothermal heat comes from hot water beneath the earth's surface. The water is heated by lava and magma under the earth's crust. We can either pump the hot water through our sinks and showers or around the house so that it warms our rooms.

We insulate our homes so that the heat we make stays in the house and isn't wasted. Insulation, like grass on the roof, or straw bales in the wall, means that our houses stay warm without using much energy.

We also have energy-efficient windows that keep the warm air inside in the winter and outside in the summer so that we don't need air conditioning.

WE GROW OUR OWN FOOD

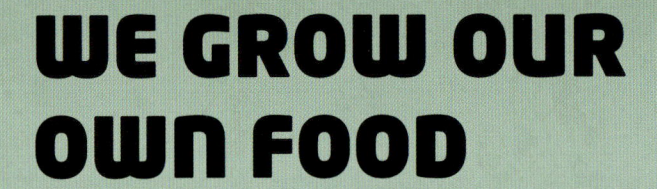

We like to grow our own food so that we can eat it as fresh as possible. Less packaging and fewer trucks moving food around is good for the planet.

People who don't have gardens of their own can use shared gardens. These are found in every community.

We try to grow the things that grow naturally at each time of the year. This is called seasonal growing. Sometimes we grow food in big greenhouses because it speeds things up and keeps plants safe from the weather.

Some things are easier to grow than others. Zucchini and carrots are easy, but some fruit is quite difficult.

WE LIVE TOGETHER AND SHARE

In the past, people sometimes didn't know their next-door neighbors. At the same time some people threw away a lot of food because they had more than they needed.

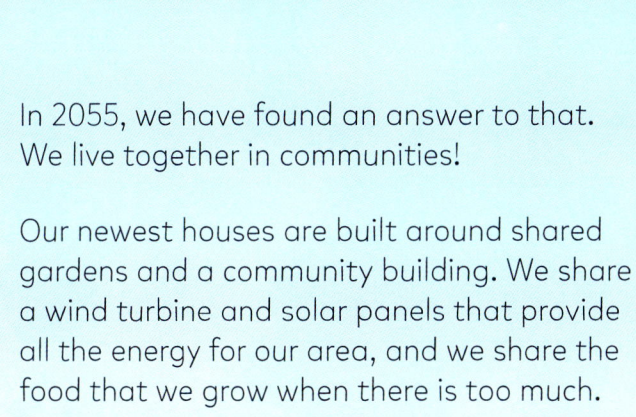

In 2055, we have found an answer to that. We live together in communities!

Our newest houses are built around shared gardens and a community building. We share a wind turbine and solar panels that provide all the energy for our area, and we share the food that we grow when there is too much.

There is always someone to play with when you come home from school and someone to help you out if you can't do something yourself.

IN 2055 OUR HOMES ARE OPEN TO FRIENDS.

29

GLOSSARY

bamboo
A type of grass which grows into long, strong tubes.

carbon dioxide
A chemical that contributes to pollution but is produced naturally in many ways, including when humans breathe!

geothermal heating
When water is heated by hot, molten rocks under the surface of the earth. This is used for heating and hot water in buildings.

graphene
A new building material that is strong but also very thin.

mycelium
A substance found in fungus that can be grown in laboratories to make a building material.

photovoltaic cells
Technology used to convert light into energy.

resin
A hard substance that comes from plants.

sandstone
Rock made from sand that has been pressed together over time and become hard.

solar panel
Several photovoltaic cells put together in a frame.

superconductor
A metal alloy that allows electricity to flow through it easily.

turbine
A rotating device which converts wind or liquid into mechanical energy.

LEARN MORE

To learn more about what cars of the future would look like, you can visit these places.

Johnson, Steven. *How We Got To Now*. New York: Viking, 2018

How Stuff Works Website
https://www.howstuffworks.com/

London Science Museum Website
https://www.sciencemuseum.org.uk/objects-and-stories/everyday-technology

National Geographic Website
https://www.nationalgeographic.co.uk/cities-of-the-future

Science Kids Website
https://www.sciencekids.co.nz/technology.html

Smithsonian Website
https://www.si.edu/Kids

INDEX

bamboo, 6

community, 26, 29

efficient, 13, 20, 21, 25

flexible, 6, 10, 16

geothermal, 24
graphene, 9

infrared, 13, 15
insulation, 5, 25

mycelium, 8

photovoltaic cells, 22
printers, 3D, 7

retina scanner, 15
robots, 17, 18, 19

sandstone, 7
solar panels, 22, 29
straw, 9, 25
sustainable, 6

turbine, 23, 29

water tank, 20
wi-fi, 12
wireless, 12